CITIZEN SCIENCE PROJECTS

Space Projects

BY IB LARSEN

Kids Core
An Imprint of Abdo Publishing
abdobooks.com

abdobooks.com

Published by Abdo Publishing, a division of ABDO, PO Box 398166, Minneapolis, Minnesota 55439.

Printed in the United States of America, North Mankato, Minnesota.
102025
012026

THIS BOOK CONTAINS RECYCLED MATERIALS

Cover Photo: Shutterstock Images
Interior Photos: Shutterstock Images, 4–5, 7, 9, 23, 28 (top), 28 (bottom), 29 (bottom); Amnaj Khetsamtip/Shutterstock Images, 10; NASA, 12–13, 17, 19, 20–21, 25, 26, 29 (top); Ben Smegelsky/NASA, 15; Scott Wiessinger/NASA, 16; Cory Huston/NASA, 24

Editors: Rebecca Higgins and Trudy Becker
Series Designer: Marley Richmond

Library of Congress Control Number: 2025939134

Publisher's Cataloging-in-Publication Data

Names: Larsen, Ib, author.
Title: Space projects / by Ib Larsen
Description: Minneapolis, Minnesota: Abdo Publishing, 2026 | Series: Citizen science projects | Includes online resources and index.
Identifiers: ISBN 9781098298593 (lib. bdg.) | ISBN 9798384932390 (ebook)
Subjects: LCSH: Science projects--Juvenile literature. | Field experiments--Juvenile literature. | Outer space--Juvenile literature. | Astronautics--Experiments--Juvenile literature. | Space sciences--Juvenile literature. | Ecology--Experiments--Juvenile literature. | Ecological science--Juvenile literature.
Classification: DDC 507.8--dc23

CONTENTS

The northern lights are often seen in northern parts of the United States, Canada, Norway, Sweden, Finland, Iceland, and Russia.

CHAPTER 1

Seeing the Northern Lights

Ali followed closely behind his father on the trail. They were hiking in Voyageurs National Park. This park is in northern Minnesota. It is far from the lights of the city where Ali lives. It was a dark night with a clear sky. The stars were very bright.

But Ali and his father were looking for more than stars. They wanted to see the northern lights.

The northern lights are natural displays of light in the night sky. They are also called aurora borealis. They occur when material from the Sun strikes Earth's air. This releases energy that is visible as the northern lights. People have

Solar Wind

Solar wind is the material from the Sun that causes the northern lights. It is different from the wind on Earth. Solar wind is made of high-energy **particles**. These particles get so hot that the Sun's gravity cannot hold them back. They shoot out into space. Sometimes the particles shoot toward Earth and create the northern lights.

Some people record what they see in the sky and share it with researchers.

watched these beautiful lights in the sky for thousands of years.

Suddenly, a green ribbon of light streaked across the sky. Ali and his father were amazed. They were seeing the northern lights! Ali's father took out a notebook. He handed it to his son. Ali wrote down the time the lights appeared. He noted their green color, and he recorded his location.

Ali and his father planned to share this information with a project run by scientists. The project is called Aurorasaurus. Its goal is to help scientists predict auroras. To do this, they need a lot of **data** about the northern lights. That is where volunteers like Ali and his father come in. By sharing their observations of the northern lights, they help the scientists running the project achieve their goals.

What Is Citizen Science?

Aurorasaurus is a citizen science project. Citizen science projects invite ordinary people to help with scientific research. Scientists design and manage these projects. But scientists cannot do all the work themselves. So they give some

Citizen scientists often need to write down what they see.

tasks to citizen scientists. This allows everyone to contribute to the research.

Many citizen science projects study space. Aurorasaurus is one example. Citizen scientists help researchers by collecting data.

Citizen scientists can compare space images using the internet.

There are many ways for volunteers to help. Some projects ask citizen scientists to look at pictures of space and find patterns. One project even allows citizen scientists to find plants that could grow in space. Without the help of citizen scientists, these projects would not be possible.

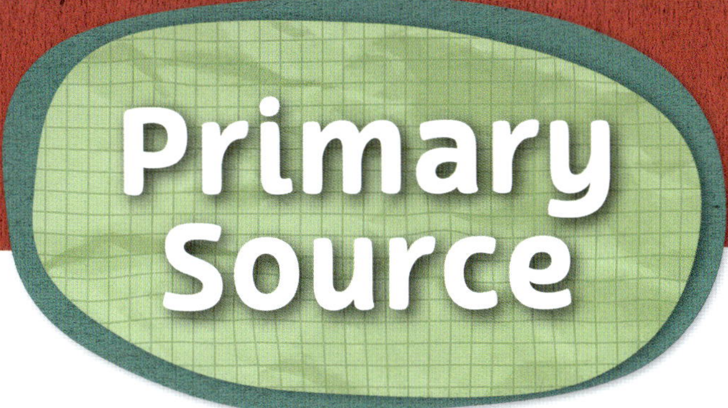

Dr. Liz MacDonald created Aurorasaurus and spoke about its importance:

> The aurora can actually be seen more widely, more often than people think. . . . We're trying to put information about when it can likely be seen in the hands of the people.

Source: Matt Hoffman. "Dr. Liz MacDonald Talks Aurora, Space Weather, and Her Citizen-Science Project, Aurorasaurus." *Science World Report*, 26 Jan. 2016, scienceworldreport.com. Accessed 23 Apr. 2025.

What's the Big Idea?

Read this quote carefully. What is its main idea? Explain how the main idea is supported by details.

One citizen science project classifies energy released by the Sun.

CHAPTER 2

Classification Projects

Citizen scientists help Aurorasaurus by collecting data themselves. But in other space projects, scientists have already collected data. Citizen scientists help with these projects by **classifying** the data.

Volunteers sort through data and label its contents. This can take a lot of time. Sometimes computers can do this, but often people need to do it. Researchers call on citizen scientists for help.

Solar Radio Burst Tracker is one example of a classification project. A solar radio burst occurs when the Sun suddenly releases a type of energy called radio waves. **Satellites** that **orbit** the Sun record these waves. But sometimes these satellites also record data unrelated to solar radio bursts. Scientists need help sorting through this data. Citizen scientists step up and help.

Citizen scientists view **graphs** created by satellites. Some of these graphs display solar

The Solar Orbiter picks up radio waves that citizen scientists look at for Solar Radio Burst Tracker.

radio bursts. Others do not. Volunteers start on the project's website by learning what a burst looks like. Then citizen scientists classify the data shown on the graphs. Their work helps scientists learn more about the Sun.

A volunteer using Backyard Worlds: Planet 9 spotted the remains of a star that had died.

Finding a New Planet?

Backyard Worlds: Planet 9 is another classification project. Citizen scientists look at pictures taken of nearby regions of space to find and identify space objects. Scientists have processed these pictures to make moving objects stand out.

Most of the objects in the space images fit in two groups. Some of the objects are small stars. Other objects are brown dwarfs.

A citizen scientist for Backyard Worlds: Planet 9 discovered a brown dwarf.

Brown dwarfs are between planets and stars in size. Some are very close to Earth's solar system.

Scientists think there is a chance that these pictures could show the solar system's ninth planet. Some scientists predict that a planet exists far beyond Neptune. Neptune is the most

Discovering Exoplanets

Citizen scientists have made major space discoveries before. Volunteers discovered at least five exoplanets in 2017. An exoplanet is a planet beyond the solar system. The citizen scientists looked at data from the Kepler space telescope. The telescope moved through space as its camera took pictures. Those citizen scientists spotted the planets in pictures.

Pluto was once thought to be the solar system's ninth planet. Scientists later discovered that Pluto is a dwarf planet.

distant known planet in the solar system. A citizen scientist could make a historic discovery by finding the ninth planet.

Explore Online

Visit the website below. Does it give any new information about a possible ninth planet that wasn't in Chapter Two?

Why Do We Think There Is a Possible Planet X?

abdocorelibrary.com/space-projects

The International Space Station (ISS) has several labs for astronauts to conduct science projects.

CHAPTER 3

Growing Plants in Space

Outer space does not seem like a place where plants could survive. Plants need air to grow. But amazingly, **astronauts** have grown plants in space. The International Space Station (ISS) is a spacecraft that orbits Earth. Astronauts live on the ISS.

They stay for months at a time. They perform experiments there. Some of those experiments focus on plants.

Astronauts grow and study plants in space for several reasons. They want to know the best ways to grow plants in space. Astronauts have even eaten the plants they have grown.

However, not every plant can grow in space. Growing Beyond Earth (GBE) studies this.

The International Space Station

The ISS is made of several parts. The first part went into space in 1998. More than 280 astronauts have visited since then. They have performed thousands of experiments. They have studied subjects such as the human body and medicine development.

Countries of the International Space Station

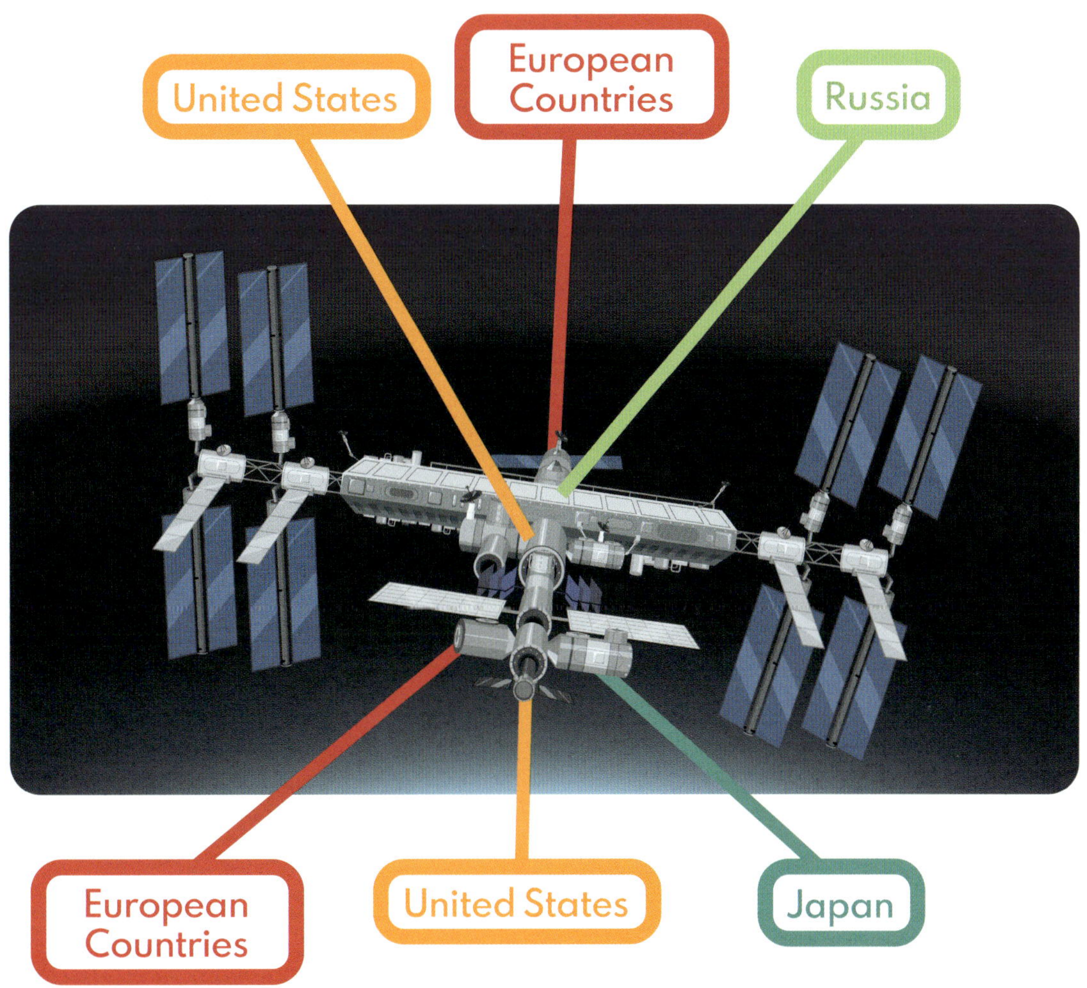

People from several different countries work together on the ISS. The first part was built by Russia. Later parts were added by other countries.

NASA has an ISS environment simulation chamber that lets plants grow on Earth in conditions that are similar to the ISS's environment.

The project tries to find the best plants for astronauts to study. Hundreds of middle and high schools across the United States participate in this project.

Scientists send schools plant **habitats** that resemble those on the ISS. They ask students to grow different kinds of plants in them. The students note how well the plants grow and how big they get. They also record how much food the plants produce. They send this data back to project scientists. The scientists use it to plan future plant experiments on the ISS.

Astronaut Mark Vande Hei grew chili peppers on the ISS in 2021.

Packaged meals on the ISS are prepared and stored so they can last a long time.

The Future of Food in Space

The GBE project gives valuable information to scientists. The project could play a role in the future of space exploration. Most of the meals astronauts eat are prepackaged. This works for stays on the ISS.

But astronauts on longer missions to places farther from Earth might need other ways of getting food. They may not have enough room on their spacecraft to hold all their food. Scientists hope that growing food crops in space will solve this problem.

GBE is just one example of a space project for citizen scientists. There are many projects that give people the chance to support space research. Citizen scientists help others learn more about the universe.

Further Evidence

Look at the website below. Does it give any new evidence to support Chapter Three?

What Do Astronauts Eat in Space?

abdocorelibrary.com/space-projects

Science Projects

Citizen scientists need to know where and how to record data for their project.

Volunteers recording the northern lights for Aurorasaurus need access to the website.

Citizen scientists identifying solar radio bursts need to know what a solar radio burst looks like and have access to the Solar Radio Burst Tracker website.

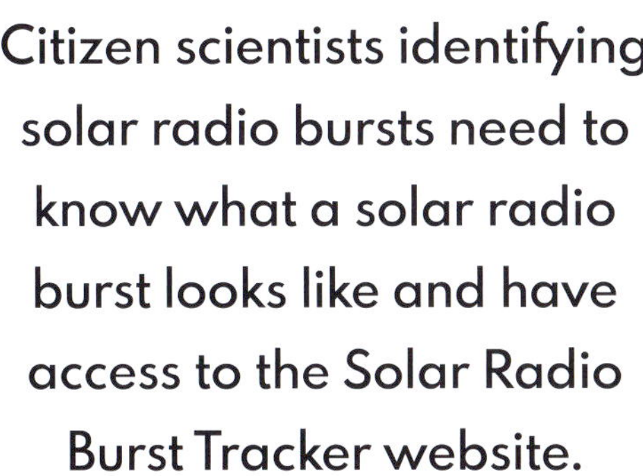

Volunteers identifying objects in pictures of space need access to a device that they can use to look at and compare images.

Glossary

astronauts
people who travel into outer space

classify
to arrange items into groups

data
information

graphs
diagrams that represent the relationship between different pieces of information

habitats
controlled environments in which a living thing can survive

orbit
to move in a round path around something

particles
very small pieces of something

satellites
human-made or natural objects that orbit larger bodies in space

Online Resources

To learn more about space projects, visit our free resource websites below.

Visit **abdocorelibrary.com** or scan this QR code for free Common Core resources for teachers and students, including vetted activities, multimedia, and booklinks, for deeper subject comprehension.

Visit **abdobooklinks.com** or scan this QR code for free additional online weblinks for further learning. These links are routinely monitored and updated to provide the most current information available.

Learn More

Beall, Abigail. *The Universe*. DK, 2024.

Behind the Scenes at the Space Stations. DK, 2022.

Huddleston, Emma. *Explore the Planets*. Abdo, 2022.

Index

About the Author

Ib Larsen is a writer and an editorial assistant living in Saint Paul, Minnesota.